F IN

English

THE BEST TEST PAPER BLUNDERS

Richard Benson

summersdale

F IN ENGLISH

Summersdale Publishers Ltd
46 West Street
Chichester
West Sussex
PO19 1RP
UK

www.summersdale.com

Printed and bound in China

ISBN: 978-1-84953-324-9

Substantial discounts on bulk quantities of Summersdale books are available to corporations, professional associations and other organisations. For details telephone Summersdale Publishers on (+44-1243-771107), fax (+44-1243-786300) or email (nicky@summersdale.com).

Contents

Introduction..5

The Classics..7

English Literature..20

English Language..31

Creative Writing..49

Poetry and Drama...65

Introduction

Did your English exams shake you up more than Shakespeare? Thousands of people have relived their exam-day nightmares with *F in Exams* and we just couldn't resist bringing you some more hilarious test paper blunders in this bite-size English edition.

This book is full to the brim with funny answers from clueless but canny students of English which will have you cackling at Coleridge, giggling at grammar, and sniggering at split infinitives. Just don't blame us if your English teacher suspects you can't speak the language…

Subject: ....**The Classics**........

Give an example of sibilance in *Romeo and Juliet*.

Juliet and Tybalt are cousins but I don't think there are any sibilance.

Give a brief summary of the plot of *The Strange Case of Dr Jekyll and Mr Hyde*.

Jekyll and Hyde find a briefcase, and it's very strange.

List the main events of *Robinson Crusoe*.

Robinson goes on a cruise.

In what way is Pip an uncertain hero?

Because he's just not sure.

Provide an example of dramatic irony in *Othello*.

What theme does the quote 'as prime as goats, as hot as monkeys' explore?

Dishes from kebab menus.

What is the overall message of *Frankenstein*?

Don't reanimate corpses.

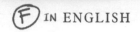

What does *Heart of Darkness* say about the nature of humanity?

It's quite dark in nature
for humans without any
electricity.

What do you think makes Mercutio such a memorable character in *Romeo and Juliet*?

He lives inside a
thermometer

Which character famously tilted at windmills?

Donkey Oatie

Paraphrase the events of *Gulliver's Travels*.

Gulliver goes on holiday. He comes back, having enjoyed himself.

What is the significance of Dr Jekyll's door in
Dr Jekyll and Mr Hyde?

It's the way he gets into Dr Jekyll's lab.

Why is isolation an important theme in Mary
Shelley's *Frankenstein*?

When you're that ugly,
isolation becomes a necessity.

Give an example of euphemism in *Midsummer Night's Dream*.

BOTTOM.

What fatal flaws did Theseus struggle with?

The flaw of the labyrinth was really slippery and dangerous.

Provide your best translation into modern English for Chaucer's lines, 'I seye for me, it is a great disese/Wher-as men han ben in greet welthe and ese/To heren of hir sodeyn fal, allas!'

Ain't it rubbish when mandem who has got loadsa dough don't got loadsa dough anymore, you get me?

Name a key theme in *Madame Bovary*.

Cows

Summarise the events of *The Fall of the House of Usher*.

Building mishaps occur.

Summarise the events of *Paradise Lost*.

God and Satan are arguing over who gets to keep Paradise, but couldn't find it anyway.

What are the main themes from *Sense and Sensibility*?

SENSES AND THE ABILITY TO SENSE THINGS.

Explore a key theme from *Wuthering Heights*.

Cliffs

List two major themes of *The Strange Case of Dr Jekyll and Mr Hyde*.

Dr Jekyll. Mr Hyde.

Subject: *English Literature*

How is Piggy made sympathetic in *The Lord of the Flies*?

His little curly tail.

To what was Hemingway referring with the quote 'This isn't fun anymore'?

This exam.

From the set texts, give two examples of Attic literature.

'How to Convert a Loft' and 'Insulation and You'.

What is the significance of the title of Orwell's *Nineteen Eighty-Four*?

That's when it was written.

List one or more characteristics of Gothic literature.

Black nail varnish.

What aspects of a text would structuralist critics look at?

The buildings.

Name one key plot device you might find in a comedy of manners.

A person who does not say 'please' and 'thank you'.

Introduce and explain one perspective of literary criticism.

Self-help books that tell you what's wrong with you and how you can improve it.

List two ways *Pride and Prejudice* can be read.

1. Sitting down, book on lap.

2. Lying down.

What conventions might show a text to be a historical novel?

Historical novels are famous novels

What does it mean when we say a novel is written in the third-person perspective?

There are only three characters.

Give an example of a proverb.

A journey of a thousand miles is as good as a rest to a blind horse that gathers no moss for want of a shoe.

Define an epistolary novel.

A novel about religious people.

lalalalala

What factors lead towards Nancy's death in *Oliver Twist*?

Charles Dickens killed her.

Discuss the reasons for the main action of *Of Mice and Men* taking place over four days.

It is a short book, so doesn't take more than four days to read.

Give one famous quote from the play *Hamlet* which makes reference to Yorick?

The grand old duke of Yorick, he had ten thousand men...

Summarise the events of Henry Fielding's *Tom Jones*.

A man becomes a famous singer.

How might the themes of *Crime and Punishment* be relevant to today's society?

It's been adapted into a TV show called Law and Order.

Name two literary genres.

Fiction and non-fiction.

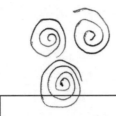

Subject: *English Language*

Name the three tenses.

Stressed, worried and concerned.

Give an example of a sentence containing a suffix.

Suffix to say, I won't be going back there again.

What is a subordinate clause?

It's a very meek clause.

Write a sentence with an example of irony.

When I put my clothes in the wash, my mum brings them back to me all irony.

Give a brief definition of a split infinitive.

When two people break up and <u>never</u> get back together.

Write a sentence containing a double negative.

Mike is ugly and he smells.

What is a relative clause?

Mrs Santa.

If someone refers to an idiolect, what do they mean?

The opposite of intellect.

When would you use a preposition?

When you want to marry someone.

Give an example of a connective.

Glue, Blu-tack or Sellotape.

Give an example of an intensifier.

My sister intensifies my feelings of annoyance.

Give an example of form.

The one you fill in to get your National Insurance card.

On average, how many words a minute do we usually speak?

It varies depending on how annoying you are.

When you articulate you:

Move your hands a lot
while you're speaking.

How significant is tone of voice when communicating?

My mum says 'it's not
what you said it's the
way that you said it.'

Give an example of a request and a gesture you might use to emphasise it.

Get lost please.

What effect does eye contact have when you are talking to someone?

It makes them think you fancy them.

Define 'multimodal' talk.

Talking to two or more models at once

What are we referring to when we refer to the 'Queen's English'?

We're referring to the fact that the Queen _is_ English (and a bit German).

Write a sentence containing a 'question tag'.

I should know what it is, shouldn't I?

Define sociolect.

A violent and dangerous individual with no empathy.

Give an example of a regional accent.

Oo arr missis

Give an example of an exchange between two people containing 'fillers'.

Two old people - their dentures will have fillers.

Define dialect.

Dr Who's biggest enemies
were the dialects.

When people from a particular class share a way of speaking it is called:

Being northern / being southern.

When people from a particular area share a way of speaking it is called:

Inside jokes.

What do we mean by 'mode'?

Grass that's been cut.

Give an example of a sentence with slang in it.

This is an example of a sentence with slang innit.

Give an example of a language routine.

Get up, speak, eat dinner, speak, go to bed.

What are anecdotes an example of?

medicine that you give someone to stop them dying of poison

 IN ENGLISH

What are we discussing when we talk about the 'flow' of a conversation?

The direction it
is moving in.

What is a sonnet?

WHAT A MOMMET AND A
POPPET GIVE BIRTH TO.

Subject: **Creative Writing**

When writing to argue, what techniques might you use to gain the readers' attention?

Writing in CAPITAL
LETTERS

You should always end a piece of argumentative writing by:

Telling the reader you
will slap them if they
refuse to agree.

What techniques might you use to gain the reader's sympathy?

Rub onion on the paper to make them cry.

What sort of newspaper article explores opinion rather than facts?

Most.

Give two stylistic features of a column.

GRECIAN. ROMAN.

What does a 'call to action' mean?

When you get made
to go to war.

Creative Writing

What is a recreation?

Sport is an example of recreation, such as tennis or yoga.

Give two techniques writers use to create atmosphere.

A few drinks.
Some good friends.

What is a 'dangling participle'?

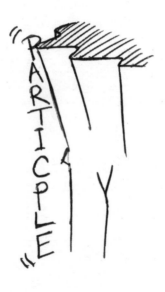

Why should an author keep their audience in mind?

Because if they kept them in real life that would be kidnapping.

Give the correct opening for writing a formal letter to a person you don't know.

Opening: 'Who are you?'

What effect can a rhetorical question have?

Irritation

What is a strap line?

When you get sunburnt wearing a strappy top and have white lines on your shoulders.

What is a headline?

The line on your head where your hat was too tight.

What sort of terms are 'you have to', 'you must' and 'you ought to'?

The sort My Mum uses too often

What is the purpose of writing to advise?

you can tell people what to do and they can't say no.

What is the effect of imperatives?

They make you poo

Give an example of an 'impersonal' instruction.

I don't know you, but
lend me a tenner.

When might you use a conditional phrase?

when washing your hair, after
the shampoo phrase.

Give an example of a group of three.

Athos, Porthos and Aramis.

Give two examples of presentational devices.

Smart board. Pointer

GAP stands for:

fashionable clothes at affordable prices.

Define 'embody'.

The thing beneath Em's head.

← Emhead
← Embody

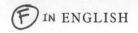

Define 'discourse marker'.

If you get any on your clothes while you're writing with it, it will wash off.

What does PEE stand for?

It's like pee, but when you're really desperate.

Give an example of a 'purpose'.

They're quite like dolphins.

Define 'ambiguity'.

The point of ambiguity is that it can't be defined.

Write a sentence that tells the reader about a character using the rule 'show don't tell'.

Subject: **Poetry and Drama**

Using the works you have studied, give an example of a heroic couplet.

BATMAN & ROBIN.

What is a roundel?

Similar to a square... but circle shaped.

How is 'Sonnet 34' a formal poem?

Because it is numbered.

What effect can alliteration have?

Makes the streets look untidy.

Give an example of a poetic form.

A poet's driving licence application.

What is a villanelle?

A place where villains go when they die.

What is a simile?

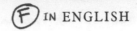

What is poetic meter?

One hundred centimetres of poem.

Give ONE example of a famous ode.

Ode cologne.

Give a brief definition of blank verse.

PAGE CONTAINING
BLANK VERSE.

PAGE

Using the set texts, discuss ONE theme shared by the poems.

They're all set texts.

Define 'physical theatre'.

A building, normally quite big, with a stage and seats and an expensive bar.

What is 'Commedia dell'arte'?

It's a high-class sitcom.

When might an author use 'anti-climax'?

It's to be used with anti-freeze.

What is melodrama?

It's the opposite of
an angry drama.

MELON-DRAMA!

In poetry, what is the 'voice'?

Someone who reads it out loud.

In poetry, what is a fourteener?

A teenage poet.

What is a stanza?

Italian book stand

Explore one work by Seigfried Sassoon.

He invented a bob in the 60s.

What is an epitaph?

A swear word.

Define repertoire.

When you keep saying the same thing over and over and over.

What does the term 'blocking' mean to a playwright?

When the characters stop each other from doing what they want to.

What themes are important to a Modernist poet?

Technology.

What is a canto?

Faster than a trot.

What made Imagist poets different to other poets writing at the time?

They drew pictures instead of writing words.

If you're interested in finding out more about our humour books, follow us on Twitter:
@SummersdaleLOL

www.summersdale.com